W9-BLR-562

THE HOUSE OF REPRESENTATIVES

THE U.S. GOVERNMENT
HOW IT WORKS

★ ★ ★

THE CENTRAL INTELLIGENCE AGENCY
THE DEPARTMENT OF HOMELAND SECURITY
THE FEDERAL BUREAU OF INVESTIGATION
THE HOUSE OF REPRESENTATIVES
THE PRESIDENCY
THE SENATE
THE SUPREME COURT

THE U.S. GOVERNMENT
HOW IT WORKS

THE HOUSE OF REPRESENTATIVES

RACHEL A. KOESTLER-GRACK

CHELSEA HOUSE
PUBLISHERS
An imprint of Infobase Publishing

The House of Representatives

Copyright © 2007 by Infobase Publishing

All rights reserved. No part of this book may be reproduced or utilized in any form or by any means, electronic or mechanical, including photocopying, recording, or by any information storage or retrieval systems, without permission in writing from the publisher. For information, contact:

Chelsea House
An imprint of Infobase Publishing
132 West 31st Street
New York, NY, 10001

ISBN-10: 0-7910-9285-2
ISBN-13: 978-0-7910-9285-9

Library of Congress Cataloging-in-Publication Data
Koestler-Grack, Rachel A., 1973-
  The House of Representatives / Rachel A. Koestler-Grack.
      p. cm. — (The U.S. government : how it works)
  Includes bibliographical references and index.
  ISBN 0-7910-9285-2 (hardcover)
1. United States. Congress. House—Juvenile literature. 2. United States.
Congress. House—History—Juvenile literature. I. Title. II. Series.

  JK1319.K64 2007
  328.73'072 — dc22

                                                2006028586

Chelsea House books are available at special discounts when purchased in bulk quantities for businesses, associations, institutions, or sales promotions. Please call our Special Sales Department in New York at (212) 967-8800 or (800) 322-8755.

You can find Chelsea House on the World Wide Web at
http://www.chelseahouse.com

Text design by James Scotto-Lavino
Cover design by Ben Peterson

Printed in the United States of America

Bang FOF 10 9 8 7 6 5 4 3 2 1

This book is printed on acid-free paper.

All links and Web addresses were checked and verified to be correct at the time of publication. Because of the dynamic nature of the Web, some addresses and links may have changed since publication and may no longer be valid.

CONTENTS

1

ATTACK ON THE HOUSE

Shortly after 2:00 in the afternoon of March 1, 1954, Lolita Lebrón and three other Puerto Rican nationalists walked through the doors of the Ladies Gallery, a balcony for visitors to the U.S. House of Representatives chamber. Lebrón had been an active advocate for Puerto Rican independence, joining the Puerto Rican Nationalist Party in the 1940s. Puerto Rico was ceded to the United States after the Spanish-American War in 1898, and in 1917, Puerto Ricans became U.S. citizens. In the early 1950s, the United States formed a commonwealth relationship with Puerto Rico. Under this agreement, Puerto Rico became a "free associated state" but was still bound to the United States for governing advice and aid. The leader of the nationalist party, Pedro Albizu Campos, thought that the relationship was a joke. To many nationalists, who wanted full independence, it seemed that the U.S. government was only "saying" that Puerto Rico was independent. In truth, Puerto Rico was still dependent on the United States. In response, Campos organized a nationalist revolt in 1950 in Puerto Rico, known as the Jayuya Uprising, and planned to assassinate President Harry S. Truman.

Eventually, Campos was arrested and sentenced to a long prison term. From prison, he began to correspond with Lebrón. He chose her, a woman he had never met, to lead a group of nationalist rebels in an attack on the U.S. House of Representatives. He picked March 1 for the attack, because on March 1, 1917—exactly 37 years earlier—the law that made Puerto Ricans U.S. citizens was enacted.

As Lebrón and her followers entered the chamber, a security guard stopped them. He asked if they had cameras, which were forbidden. He never even thought to check them for guns. The four visitors took their seats in the back row of the gallery, anticipating the moment of action. At the time, the House was busy voting on a bill to permit Mexican farm laborers to work in the country for temporary employment. House Speaker Joseph Martin had just finished counting the "ayes." There were 168.

Suddenly, Lebrón stood up and screamed, "Viva Puerto Rico libre!" ("Long live free Puerto Rico!") As she waved the Puerto Rican flag, the other three followers pulled out guns and riddled 29 shots across the House floor.

This photograph of the floor of the House of Representatives was taken from the approximate spot where four Puerto Rican nationalists fired onto the congressmen below. Five representatives were wounded in the attack on March 1, 1954.

One bullet ricocheted off the desk of the majority leader, Charles Halleck.

CONGRESSMEN SHOT

The House erupted in chaos. Some members bolted for the doors. Others dropped to the floor. All the while, the nationalists randomly fired off shots. Several members were struck as they fled the room. One representative took a shot in the right shoulder. He stumbled through the door and toppled over. "He got me in the back," he groaned. A representative from Michigan was hit with multiple bullets in the chest and abdomen.

Representative James Van Zandt crawled into the coat room and from there, managed to escape the chamber. He raced up the stairs to the gallery. With the help of spectators and security guards, he managed to over-power the rebels. Although none of the nationalists expected to make it out alive, all four were arrested un-harmed and later imprisoned. Luckily, all five wounded representatives recovered.

The next day, the House held its regular session. About 200 members showed up, an unusually large turnout for this point in the session. The House members wanted to send a message to other radical groups. Congress would not tolerate any kind of assault. The members refused to let the would-be assassins get their way and keep the House from conducting its business.

Naturally, a number of bills were proposed to increase security in the House chamber, including one suggestion to install bulletproof glass between the gallery and the floor. No action, though, was taken. Instead, a bill was passed that made it a felony for any unauthorized person to carry a weapon anywhere on the Capitol grounds. Anyone caught breaking the law would be punished with a $10,000 fine and 10 years in prison.

The Capitol police held three of the four Puerto Rican nationalists in custody soon after they opened fire in the House of Representatives. At left is Lolita Lebrón; the man at center is Rafael Cancel Miranda; and the man at right is Andres Figueroa Cordero. The four nationalists went to the Capitol expecting to die, but they were all arrested unharmed.

When people think about the House of Representatives, stories like this one probably do not pop into mind. Most people have the idea that government is all about dull meetings, long discussions, and dirt-digging campaigns. The House of Representatives, however, has played an active role in some of the most exciting and dramatic moments in U.S. history. Sometimes, the actions of the House were heroic. Sometimes, the House played the villain. But throughout more than 200 years of being in the political limelight, the House of Representatives has endured as the keeper of democracy. It stands guard in front of the Constitution, guaranteeing a government that is ruled by the people.

2

First Steps

As the sun peaked over the Atlantic Ocean on March 4, 1789, guns at the New York City Battery shattered the still morning. An 11-gun salute announced the inauguration, or formal dedication, of the new U.S. government. Church bells peeled, adding to the excitement. Later that morning, both houses of Congress would meet to count the electoral ballots from each state and declare the first president of the United States. Everyone knew, however, that George Washington—the great hero of the American Revolution—would be the winner. Across the country, he was so loved and respected that the idea of anyone else as president was unthinkable. Still, the breeze in New York City that day must have been charged with anticipation.

These expectations deflated when only 13 of the 65 members of the House showed up on that first day. Because 30 members were needed to perform business, all those present could do was agree to meet the following morning and adjourn. Travel troubles had delayed some congressmen. In those days, people traveled across the country by horse over crude, rough roads. Sometimes no roads existed at all. Many congressmen had to travel hundreds of miles, even a thousand miles, to get to New York. A simple rainstorm could postpone travel for an entire day.

This lithograph shows Federal Hall (at the end of the street) in the 1790s. The first session of the U.S. Congress was held at Federal Hall in New York City. The House of Representatives hoped to begin work on March 4, 1789, but it did not achieve a quorum of its members untill April 1.

On April 1, 1789, a thirtieth member of the House showed up at Federal Hall, then the home of Congress. Finally, the House had a quorum and could start business. Some members were nervous about inaugurating the House on April Fool's Day, but it was time to move forward. Five days later, the Senate gained a quorum as well, and Congress was now ready to count the electoral ballots. Once that was accomplished, a messenger was sent to inform Washington of his election officially.

Washington finally arrived in New York on April 23, and a week later, his inauguration was held. When the moment finally came, Washington stepped out onto a second-story balcony of Federal Hall. On the street below, the fidgeting crowd, catching a glimpse of its new leader, greeted him with deafening cheers. New York Chancellor Robert R. Livingston held up a Bible and began the oath as written in the Constitution. "Do you solemnly swear," he said, "that you will faithfully execute the office of President of the United States, and will, to the best of your ability, preserve, protect, and defend the Constitution of the United States?"

"I solemnly swear," Washington replied. He then repeated the oath and bowed down and kissed the Bible.

"It is done," Livingston shouted. "Long live George Washington, president of the United States." The crowd roared with excitement as cannons boomed in the harbor. This event marked the beginning of a government that had a bold and bright future few could have even imagined.

After the ceremony, people in the streets slowly dispersed. The members of Congress returned to their

This drawing depicts George Washington arriving by barge in New York for his inauguration in 1789. Once the House and Senate had quorums, they tallied the electoral votes that declared Washington to be the nation's first president. Messengers were sent to tell Washington, who then journeyed from his home at Mount Vernon in Virginia to New York.

meeting rooms in Federal Hall. Naturally, members were full of pride and hope as they set out to test their new government. They also must have been uneasy. After all, eyes around the world were watching this brave little country. Some wondered if a democracy could stand the test of time. Others hoped it would crumble so they could swoop in and take control.

THE DYNAMIC DUO

To many people, the U.S. House of Representatives is the greatest decision-making body in history. The House is an extraordinary tool that passes laws for the American people. Because House members serve only two-year terms, new representatives constantly bring in fresh ideas that reflect the popular demands of the people. From the first election in 1789 to the present, all House members have been elected. Not one has ever been appointed. For this reason, many people refer to the House of Representatives as the "People's House." The purpose of the House is to give the American people a voice in Congress.

To understand why the House was created, it is important to understand what caused Americans to create their own government in the first place. Before Americans won independence, Great Britain ruled the colonies. The American colonists did not have any say in the laws that the British Parliament passed for them. Colonists wanted American representatives in Parliament so they could offer their own opinions. When Parliament refused to listen to the colonists, the Americans decided to fight for independence. After the colonists won the Revolutionary War, they were faced with the challenge of creating their own government. It was a huge and daunting task.

On May 14, 1787, the Founding Fathers gathered around a table at Independence Hall in Philadelphia, Pennsylvania. With quill in hand and ink jar filled, they began to work on Article I of the United States

BRANCHES OF THE U.S. GOVERNMENT

The federal government has three branches—the legislative, the executive, and the judicial. Each branch has some authority and power of its own and some power to regulate the other two branches. In turn, each has some of its power controlled by the other two.

Congress is the legislative branch of the federal government. It is divided into the House of Representatives and the Senate. Even though each house has separate duties, the consent of both bodies is required to pass a law.

The executive branch consists of the president and his delegates. The president is both the head of state and the head of government. He also serves as commander-in-chief of the military and chief diplomat to other countries. According to the Constitution, the president must "take care that the laws be faithfully executed." The president manages national affairs and the work of the federal government. In addition, he or she has important legislative and judicial powers. The president signs or vetoes bills, has the power to pardon criminals convicted of federal crimes, and appoints Supreme Court justices and federal judges.

The second-highest executive official is the vice president. If the president dies, resigns, or is removed from office, the vice president

Constitution. This section created the legislative, or lawmaking, branch of government—better known as the U.S. Congress. Remembering their frustration with Great Britain, the Founding Fathers wanted to make sure that the United States had a government run by the people. They were so dedicated to this belief that

takes over. This situation has happened nine times in U.S. history. The vice president also serves as president of the Senate and has the power to break any tie votes in that chamber. The executive branch also includes the heads of various departments who serve as a council of advisors to the president known as the Cabinet.

The nine-justice Supreme Court is the highest court in the judicial branch. The court mainly deals with matters related to the federal government, disputes between states, and interpretations of the U.S. Constitution. The Supreme Court can declare any legislative or executive action as unconstitutional, canceling the law or halting further action.

The federal judicial system consists of the Supreme Court and various lower courts, including the U.S. Courts of Appeals and the U.S. District Courts. Separate but not totally independent of the federal judicial system are individual state court systems—each dealing with its own laws and judicial rules. The Supreme Court of each state is the final authority on interpreting that state's laws and constitution. A case can be appealed to a federal court, but only if it concerns an issue about the U.S. Constitution or U.S. laws and treaties.

the very first words of the Constitution read, "We the people of the United States ..."

In Article I, the 55 delegates of the Constitutional Convention created the guidelines for Congress. They decided that each state must have its own representatives to voice the concerns of the people who live there. But they could not agree on how each state should be represented. States with a large number of residents wanted representation based on population. Of course, smaller states did not like this idea. With fewer members, they feared they would not have a fair voice. Instead, they wanted equal representation for each state.

The argument continued until it was settled by the Great Compromise. The delegates at the convention agreed that Congress would consist of two chambers—the Senate and the House of Representatives, or House. In the House, members would be elected based on the population of each state. The greater the population, the more representatives a state would have. In the Senate, each state would seat two senators, regardless of population.

Many people see the Senate and the House as two separate entities. In truth, they are closely knit, forming the dynamic duo of U.S. law. The main job of Congress is to pass federal laws, including laws on taxes, government budgets, and trade. It has other powers as well. Congress has the power to declare war on other countries. At times, it may conduct investigations on certain questionable foreign policy activities or on some issue that has caused problems in the United States.

Although the Senate and the House are equal partners in the lawmaking realm, each has some separate duties. The Senate ratifies treaties that the president makes with other countries. For a treaty to be approved, two-thirds of the Senate must vote in favor of it. Also, the Senate confirms presidential appointments. Presidents nominate important government officials, like Supreme Court justices, ambassadors, heads of government departments and agencies, and top military leaders. The Senate must approve nominees by a majority vote. If the Senate does not approve a nominee, the president must pick someone else for the job.

The Constitution gives the House of Representatives three special duties. First, the House has the exclusive

Delegates to the Constitutional Convention in Philadelphia gathered for the signing of the U.S. Constitution in 1787. With the Great Compromise, the delegates agreed that Congress would have two chambers—the House of Representatives, in which members would be elected based on the population of each state, and the Senate, in which each state would have two members. The compromise eased the fears of both large states and small states.

right to introduce and control bills about finance, taxes, and government spending. Also, the House can impeach a federal official who is suspected of misconduct. Impeachment is a rarely used power; in these cases, the House draws up the charges and presents them to the Senate. The Senate then acts as the jury in a trial. If a president is facing an impeachment trial, the chief justice of the Supreme Court serves as the judge. In order to impeach an official, two-thirds of the Senate must find the accused guilty of the charges.

The final special task of the House pops up during quirky election years. If no presidential candidate wins the majority of electoral votes, the House chooses the president. This situation has happened twice. Likewise, if no candidate for vice president wins the majority of electoral votes, the Senate elects the winner.

Throughout the summer of 1787, delegates spent long hours wrestling with the issues of creating a new government. Undoubtedly, there were arguments and debates, additions, deletions, and revisions. On September 17, the Convention held its final meeting, completing the Constitution. Although the delegates knew there would probably be amendments, or additions and changes, to the document, they believed the Constitution clearly stated the type of government Americans wanted. Delegates then sent a copy to each of the 13 states for their approval. In 1788, the U.S. Constitution was ratified, and the first Congress was scheduled to meet in New York City in 1789.

3

Early Successes

At the first meeting of Congress in 1789, members stared wide-eyed at a towering mountain of tasks. The Constitution set up few guidelines for the executive and judicial departments of government. The powers and duties of those branches had to be determined by Congress. The House concentrated on the executive departments, and the Senate focused on the judicial branch.

Congress also had to begin to discuss amendments to the Constitution, including a Bill of Rights. Acting as the House floor manager, James Madison pushed to get them rolling, especially those that would limit the power of the federal government and protect personal liberties. These amendments—known as the Bill of Rights—were important to the American people. Several states agreed to ratify the Constitution only if a Bill of Rights was added. So naturally, it was a matter of top priority.

At times, the debates over the amendments became so heated that Madison had to pound his gavel and call everyone to order. The proposed amendments would protect basic human rights, such as freedom of speech, freedom of the press, the freedom to gather as a group, freedom of religion, the right to a fair trial, and the right to bear arms. They also prohibited cruel and unusual punishment and unlawful search and seizure—instead requiring authorities to have a proper search warrant to enter someone's property. The Fifth Amendment protects witnesses in criminal cases. A person may "plead the Fifth" if he thinks his testimony will make him look guilty of a crime.

By August 24, House members had agreed to 17 amendment proposals, which they grouped as a Bill of Rights. The package went to the Senate for approval or rejection. In the Senate, the amendments were combined or cut until only 12 remained. Just in the nick of time on September 28, the day before the first session ended, Congress sent the amendments to the 13 states for approval. Not until December 15, 1791, did the states ratify 10 of the 12 amendments. These 10 amendments became the Bill of Rights. The other two amendments, regarding salaries of congressmen and how to distribute House seats, failed to pass. Interestingly, the amendment on salaries proposed in 1789 was finally ratified in 1992 as the Twenty-Seventh Amendment to the Constitution.

RAISING REVENUE

One of the most pressing issues at the first session was the need for money. At this point, the government had

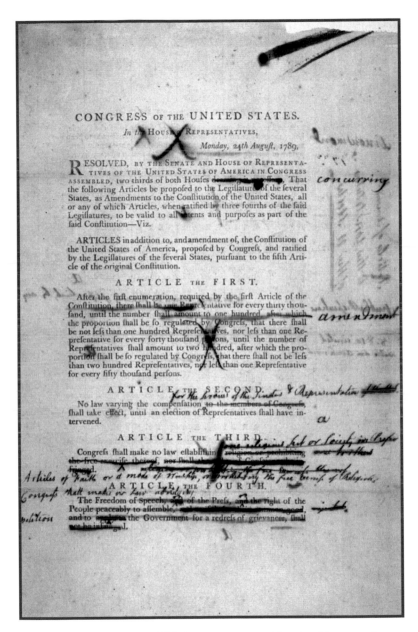

This draft of the Bill of Rights, as passed by the House of Representatives, contains editing changes made in the Senate. The draft is dated August 24, 1789. On the day before the end of its first session, Congress sent 12 amendments to the states for their approval.

absolutely nothing, except a hefty $50 million debt run up during and after the Revolutionary War. The Congress in place before 1788 had no power to raise money. Instead, it relied on the states to pay its bills. In the beginning, states frequently refused to pay their share or simply did not have the money to do so. Often, states paid less than what Congress requested. Under the Constitution, Congress now had the power to pass tax laws. Citizens would be required under law to pay taxes. The money, or revenue, raised by taxes would pay the debt and help run the government.

All revenue laws must begin in the House. Therefore, House members proposed a series of bills to raise money for the government. Naturally, certain representatives fought to protect their citizens from taxes that would weaken their economies. For example, one representative suggested a $10 tax on every imported slave. Members from Southern states leaped to their feet in angry protest, because Southerners relied on slaves to work their large plantations. Likewise, New Englanders opposed any tax on imported molasses since they used molasses to make rum.

On the other hand, some citizens wanted taxes on all imports. In the early Congresses, one way to get a bill passed in the House was through petitions filed by individuals or groups that were seeking aid or protection. Each request went to a specific committee for consideration. Often, the request was met with appropriate legislation. These first petitions helped the House understand the needs of its

As a member of the House of Representatives, James Madison was instrumental in getting the Bill of Rights passed. He avoided having the House take up a discussion on where the permanent capital would be, knowing it would cause strife and delay action on more important issues.

THE FEDERAL CITY

★ ★ ★ ★ ★

In its second session, Congress did reach agreement on the site of the nation's new capital. On July 16, 1790, Congress founded the District of Columbia, a federal district carved from land ceded by Maryland and Virginia. The city was originally designed by Pierre Charles L'Enfant, whose initial plan was to build it in a diamond shape measuring 10 miles (16 kilometers) on each side. Later, the portion of the diamond that was in Virginia was returned to that state. The city plan was surveyed by Andrew Ellicott and Benjamin Banneker, a free-born African American who was a mathematician and an astronomer. In 1791, the site was named Washington, after the nation's first president. Out of modesty, however, George Washington always referred to it as "the Federal City." Congress would have ultimate authority over the district, even though it gave some limited rule to the municipal government. All three branches of the federal government are centered in Washington, D.C., as are the headquarters of most federal agencies.

The first cornerstone of the White House was laid in October 1792, and the building was completed in 1800. Soon after, John Adams became the first president to live in the White House. The Capitol building

constituents—or voters. They also reinforced the purpose of the House—to consider the concerns of the citizens.

The first petition discussed by the House came from the tradesmen and manufacturers of Baltimore, Maryland. They asked for a tax on all imported goods that could be made in the United States. This tax would encourage citizens to buy American products instead of products made

also opened to Congress in 1800. But the district's darkest hour loomed ahead. During the War of 1812, British forces stormed the city, burning public buildings, including the Capitol, the Treasury building, and the White House.

Washington, D.C., was rebuilt to be bolder and grander. For many years, though, the city remained more like a small town. When the population finally grew larger, Congress passed the Twenty-Third Amendment, allowing Washington, D.C., to have votes in the Electoral College. Today, the city has nearly 600,000 residents. Besides the White House and the Capitol, many national monuments also adorn the U.S. capital city. These include the Washington Monument, the Jefferson Memorial, the Lincoln Memorial, the Franklin Delano Roosevelt Memorial, the District of Columbia War Memorial, the National World War II Memorial, the Albert Einstein Memorial, the Korean War Veterans Memorial, and the Vietnam Veterans Memorial. Washington, D.C., is also home to the world-famous Smithsonian Institution, an education and research institution with 19 museums and nine research centers. Hundreds of thousands of Americans visit the capital each year to get a little taste of the nation's history.

in foreign countries. The long list included soap, cheese, candles, boots, leather gloves, saddles, clothing, and even pickled fish.

After considering both sides during scrappy debates, the House passed a revenue bill that taxed all imported goods, except a list of items that had a specific tax amount. To enforce the laws, the House also passed a collection bill that designated certain ports of entry into the United States. In those days, manufacturers shipped their products by boat. Imported goods could only pass through these specific ports. The bill also created a force of 100 federal officials who had the power to search incoming ships and collect the appropriate duties.

SEARCH FOR A HOME

Another troublesome topic that kept arising was where the new government would make its permanent home. During the Revolution, the government moved from place to place. Until this time, it had seemed more like an orphan, relying on the hospitality of parent cities. In 1785, the government settled in New York. Naturally, New Yorkers, seeing financial benefits in being the capital, hoped it would stay there. No commitment had been made, however, and the Constitution said nothing about the seat of government.

Congress was pulled in several directions. Many representatives thought the government should move to Philadelphia, Pennsylvania. The city was near the center of the 13 states. Also, the Declaration of Independence and the Constitution had been written there. It seemed appropriate that the government should reside where these monumental documents were born. Southerners pushed for a location farther south, on the Potomac River. Still others lobbied for Trenton, New Jersey, because the government was briefly seated there in 1784.

At the first session of Congress, James Madison dodged the discussion. He knew it would trigger controversy and might delay more pressing issues. It quickly became clear, however, that the government would need a separate piece of land set aside as a federal district. This way, Congress could have full jurisdiction to govern the city. Anywhere else, Congress would have only a limited amount of authority. The first session ended on September 29, 1789, without final action on the matter.

The first session turned out to be a tremendous success. The House secured revenue, established the executive departments of the government, created a judicial system for the United States, and wrote a Bill of Rights. Of course, members disagreed and even quarreled at times. The arguments, though, never got to the point where they caused divisions in the House. House members were determined to make the Constitution work. Deep down, some representatives worried that it might fail. The U.S. government was the first of its kind. No other country had dared to try a democracy. If it crumbled, foreign governments would mock the Americans for creating a republic. Worse, it might prove the common belief that it was impossible to build a lasting government based on liberty, justice, and protection of private property. Cooperation between House members was crucial in the beginning. They would have to work together to make this experiment in freedom a success. The second session was only four months away, and representatives would soon learn that, in the business of politics, teamwork is tough.

4

A HOUSE DIVIDED

The harmony and unity that characterized the House during the opening session quickly faded. Regional differences, committee disagreements, and clashes of opinion soon developed among members. Before long, the House began to divide into opposing camps. At times, the tug-of-war was so fierce that it threatened to tear the Union apart. These early face-offs were the first seeds of political parties taking root.

The second session was scheduled to open on Monday, January 4, 1790. As during the first Congress, the House lacked a quorum, not achieving one until January 7. The first item up for consideration was the "Report on Public Credit." Secretary of the Treasury Alexander Hamilton had put together this report on the national debt. The report revealed that the national debt was at a staggering $54,124,464.56, about $12 million of which was owed to foreigners, mostly the French and the Dutch. In the report, Hamilton recommended that the federal government pick up the remaining state debts, which would add up to $25 million to the national debt. He suggested the government raise money to pay for these debts by passing an excise tax—an extra tax on select items like liquor and tobacco.

Immediately, the report sparked controversy in the House. Paying off the national debt was one thing, but to take on the state debts was quite another. Some of the states—mostly Southern—had paid off most of their debts. Other states had barely made a dent in repaying their debts. By picking up the tab, the government seemed to be penalizing the states that had faithfully made their payments and rewarding the ones that had not.

The proposal contained another obstacle. The federal portion of the debt had been racked up by borrowing money to purchase supplies during the war. At that time, the government also issued certificates to pay the army. The certificates were like bonds, which soldiers could later cash in with interest. Until this point, the government had been unable to buy back these certificates. Soldiers and widows of soldiers desperately needing money sold them to other buyers, often at a low price. The government now promised to buy back these certificates. Second-hand buyers would cash in the certificates for a profit, while the original holders who sold their certificates would gain nothing.

James Madison boldly opposed Hamilton's proposal. He insisted that the original holders, such as soldiers

Proposals made by Alexander Hamilton, the secretary of
the treasury, to address the national debt stirred up the first
rifts in the House of Representatives. A divide between the
Northern states and the Southern states was forming.

and patriotic merchants who had provided food and supplies during the war, be awarded the full value of the certificates. The buyers looking for a quick buck, he said, should get less. He argued that Congress should not forget the people who really deserved the payment. He also opposed picking up the state debts, which he felt was another example of injustice. He may have had a bias on this issue, however, because his home state of Virginia had been paying its debts.

The trouble with Madison's argument was that it would be nearly impossible to know which certificate holders were original and which were secondary. So his motion to award the certificates in different amounts was defeated by a vote of 36 to 13. Although this landslide defeat crushed Madison, many people around the country applauded his efforts. One newspaper reporter praised Madison as "fearless of the blood suckers" and willing to stand up and fight for "the rights of widows and orphans, the original creditors and the war worn soldier."

Madison, though, fared better on the issue of picking up state debts. The House rejected Hamilton's proposal by a vote of 31 to 29—a two-vote difference. As soon as they heard the results, Hamilton and his supporters broke down in tears. One representative from Massachusetts stood up in frustration. His state should not have to bear such intolerable financial burdens, he shouted, burdens that came from winning freedom and independence.

After this debate, representatives could see the House dividing into two parties, which became known as the

Federalists and the Anti-Federalists. To make the dissension worse, a petition arose over an issue that would plague the United States for the next 70 years and ultimately tear it in two.

FINDING A COMPROMISE

About this time, Quakers from New York and Philadelphia petitioned Congress to abolish the slave trade, the buying and selling of slaves. The Pennsylvania Abolition Society went one step further and demanded that all slavery be abolished. The petition was signed by the society's president, Benjamin Franklin. Instantly, tempers in the House erupted. Southerners threatened that any discussion of ending slavery would jeopardize the Union. They quoted Bible passages to defend their right to own slaves. On the other side, Northerners held up the Declaration of Independence to support their arguments. Some members suggested a gradual emancipation, or freeing, of slaves with a compensation of money to the slaveholders. How to raise money to fund this proposal provoked even more arguments.

The House had reached a critical moment in history. Several issues still needed to be resolved, including agreement on a temporary and permanent location for the national capital, and Northern congressmen kept bringing up petitions against slavery. A definite line between North and South was emerging. There was even talk about dissolving the Union and starting over. In addition, Madison claimed that some members had sworn to oppose all further proposals on the debt unless the assumption of state debts was included. If a compromise was not found, the Union would be in grave danger.

While House members stomped their feet and pounded their fists, Thomas Jefferson was arriving in New York to begin his duties as secretary of state. Jefferson knew little about the issues boiling in Congress. He was on his way to meet the president when he bumped into Hamilton on the street. As the two men walked to Washington's home, Hamilton fumed about the House debates. When they arrived at the door, Hamilton paced back and forth for a half-hour, rambling on about the divided House and the danger of secession from either the Northern states or the Southern states. Hamilton begged Jefferson to help resolve the crisis.

Jefferson invited him to dinner the next day and assured him that, with some sacrifices, a compromise could be found to save the Union. Jefferson invited Madison to join them. At dinner, Jefferson pointed out that picking up state debts would be a bitter sacrifice for Southerners. He then made a suggestion that might sweeten the blow. Northerners could agree to house the capital in Philadelphia for 10 years. Then it would move permanently to a site along the Potomac River. The compromise could be made if two Virginia members would change their votes on the state-debts issue and if Hamilton gained support from Northern members for the Potomac capital location. Madison agreed to the arrangement but added that he would never vote in support of assuming state debts. He would not be too loud in his opposition, however.

Naturally, some members were infuriated by each decision, but the compromise went through. Everyone did agree that the capital should be named Washington, in honor of the nation's first president. As for the name of the district, commissioners of the project decided to use the name of the man credited with discovering America—Christopher Columbus. President Washington selected the precise spot for the District of Columbia on the Potomac, a 100-square-mile (about 260-square-kilometer) piece of land carved out of Virginia and Maryland. Later in 1847, the area south of the Potomac was returned to Virginia.

The agreement did not relieve all the tension, but it was reduced to a simmer for the time being. The second session ended on August 12, 1790, with the Union still together, but certain trouble looming.

THE REVOLUTION OF 1800

For the first and only time in American history, the election of 1800 pitted the president (John Adams) against the vice president (Thomas Jefferson). The election was so hostile it is sometimes referred to as the "Revolution of 1800."

The trouble started brewing after the previous election. The presidential election of 1796 was the first one to elect a president from one ticket and a vice president from the other. The outcome exposed a flaw in the Constitution's original Electoral College: Each elector cast two votes for president. The person who won the majority of electoral votes would be president; the runner-up would be vice president. The system did not address presidential and vice presidential candidates running on the same ticket. In the election of 1796, Federalist John Adams and his running mate, Thomas Pinckney, were on one ticket. Democratic-Republican Thomas Jefferson and Aaron Burr were on the other. Adams won the majority of the votes and the presidency. However, Jefferson—a candidate of the opposing party—received the second-most votes and became vice president.

By 1800, the Federalist Party's loyalties were a mess. Adams, the incumbent president, was attacked by the opposition and disliked within his own Federalist Party. Therefore, Federalist leader Alexander Hamilton schemed to get the vice presidential candidate, Charles Cotesworth Pinckney, elected instead. On the other ticket, Jefferson was again running with Burr.

Mudslinging marred the campaign. The Federalists claimed that the Democratic-Republicans, who had evolved from the Anti-Federalists, were radicals who would murder opponents, burn churches, and destroy the government. Likewise, the Democratic-Republicans accused Adams of planning to declare himself king and make a dynasty-like alliance with Great Britain.

When it came time to vote, something unexpected happened. With one state left to vote, the election was tied 65 to 65 in the Electoral College. The remaining state—South Carolina—cast eight votes for the Democratic-Republicans, giving the election to Jefferson and Burr. There was a twist, however. Each elector cast two votes. The Democratic-Republicans cast one vote each for

Artist Rembrandt Peale painted this portrait of Thomas Jefferson in 1800, the year in which he ran a bitter race against John Adams to be president. The election pointed out flaws in the Electoral College, when Jefferson and his running mate, Aaron Burr, tied with the most votes. The election went to the House of Representatives, which voted 36 times before Jefferson finally won.

Jefferson and Burr. Therefore, the split votes resulted in a tie between Jefferson and Burr.

In the event of a tie, the Constitution states that the final election will take place in the House of Representatives. At this point, the Federalists controlled the House, and the Democratic-Republicans were in the minority. This situation muddied an already messy election.

DEADLOCK

On February 11, 1801, Congress members trudged through a howling snowstorm on their way to the Capitol. The House gathered in the library to vote for president. The members agreed that they would not adjourn until a decision had been made. Hamilton hated the idea of Burr becoming president. For weeks, he had been writing to Federalist friends, urging them to vote for Jefferson. He did not particularly like Jefferson, but he saw Burr as a man who was interested only in his own power. To Hamilton, Jefferson was far less dangerous than Burr.

On the first ballot, Jefferson took eight states—New York, New Jersey, Virginia, Pennsylvania, North Carolina, Georgia, Kentucky, and Tennessee. Burr had six—Massachusetts, New Hampshire, Rhode Island, Connecticut, Delaware, and South Carolina. Two states—Vermont and Maryland—were split. Since a candidate needed to win nine states, the House voted again. All day, through the night, and into the next morning, the House continued to vote. Each time, the result was the same. Apparently, Hamilton had not persuaded the New England states to vote

ANOTHER HOUSE PRESIDENT

The Revolution of 1800 brought a strange new era to Congress—several years of a single-party government. After the election of 1800, the Federalist Party fell apart, leaving only the Democratic-Republican Party to carry on.

In 1824, the Democratic-Republican Party splintered into four separate camps for the presidency. One faction was led by candidate Andrew Jackson, the charismatic hero of the War of 1812 and a former U.S. representative and senator. Another candidate was John Quincy Adams, the secretary of state and son of former President John Adams. William Crawford, the current secretary of the treasury and former secretary of war, also ran for the presidency, along with Henry Clay, the Speaker of the House who was known as "The Great Compromiser."

Although Andrew Jackson won the popular vote, none of the candidates had clinched the necessary majority of electoral votes. Therefore, the presidential election was thrown to the House. Only the top three Electoral College candidates are considered by the House of Representatives, so the remaining candidates were Jackson, Adams, and Crawford.

Clay's supporters shifted to Adams, whose position on certain policies was closest to Clay's. Adams won on the first House ballot. All along, Jackson had expected to sweep the election because he had won the popular vote and had the most electoral votes the first time around. When he heard about Adams's victory, he was stunned. Jackson, though, would eventually have his revenge. Four years later, he again ran against Adams, and in that election, he won.

for Jefferson. Perhaps the representatives hoped to force a whole new election. For whatever reason, they refused to change their votes. Finally at midnight on February 12, after 28 failures, House members decided to adjourn and begin the balloting again at 11:00 the next morning.

Day after day, members repeated the vote with no change. The House was deadlocked. As tensions rose, some members worried that the crisis would cause the government to collapse.

Finally on February 14, Delaware Federalist James Bayard announced that he would end the contest by voting for Jefferson. Perhaps Hamilton influenced his decision. Or maybe Bayard wanted to stop the election from becoming a national catastrophe. Two days passed, though, and he had not yet made good on his word. Some dealing was going on between the Federalists and the Democratic-Republicans. On February 17, the Vermont representative withdrew, and his replacement voted for Jefferson. Some representatives from Maryland cast blank votes, allowing Jefferson to win that state. Delaware and South Carolina both cast blank votes. The New England states—Massachusetts, New Hampshire, Rhode Island, and Connecticut—stuck with Burr till the bitter end. The final vote gave Jefferson 10 states and Burr four. After 36 ballots and seven weary days, the House at last elected Thomas Jefferson as president.

In December 1803, Congress proposed the Twelfth Amendment, requiring electors to cast one vote for president and a separate vote for vice president. The amendment was ratified the following year.

In a little more than a decade, the House of Representatives had already used two of its special powers—initiating revenue bills and deciding a tied election. Although the House discussed financial issues at every session, few members probably thought they would ever see a tied election. Just one of the three exclusive rights remained untouched—impeachment of a federal official.

5

WAR IN CONGRESS

Georgia, as well as many other Southern states, lay in ruins. General William Sherman of the Union Army had carved a path of destruction from Atlanta to Savannah, 300 miles long and 60 miles wide (483 kilometers long and 97 kilometers wide). Plumes of smoke and puffs of ash still rose from the charred skeletons of buildings and plantations when the Confederate Army surrendered on April 9, 1865. After four years of battle and 600,000 dead, Southerners put down their guns and admitted defeat, bringing an end to the Civil War. At long last, the Union could begin to heal, but the war left stinging wounds on both sides. Bitter grudges and suspicions poisoned the hearts of Congress members. What was meant to be a long-awaited reunion actually sparked a whole new war, this time in Congress.

Five days after the Confederacy surrendered, President Abraham Lincoln and his wife attended a special performance of the comedy *Our American Cousin* at Ford's Theatre in Washington, D.C. Undoubtedly, with the war behind him, Lincoln needed some diversion to take his mind off the heavy task of rebuilding the South. After all, the worst was behind him, he must have thought. During the third act of the play, a man named John Wilkes Booth burst through the curtains of the presidential box and shot Lincoln in the back of the head at point-blank range.

President Abraham Lincoln was fatally shot by John Wilkes Booth on April 14, 1865, in Ford's Theatre in Washington, D.C. Lincoln was killed just days after the Civil War ended. The assassination could not have come at a worse time—the war may have been over, but the nation was still in disarray.

The president slumped forward. The bullet had entered near his left ear and had lodged behind his right eye. He died the following morning.

President Lincoln's sudden death shocked the nation. It was the first assassination of a president in U.S. history and could not have come at a worse time. The war may have ended, but the country was in shambles. Who would nurse the haggard nation back to health?

Under the Constitution, the vice president takes over if the president is killed or dies. In this instance, Vice President Andrew Johnson was sworn in as the new president. Many congressmen were relieved to have Johnson in office. He seemed like just the man to whip the South back into shape. They could not have been more mistaken.

BUTTING HEADS

Soon after taking office, President Johnson issued two proclamations for re-establishing loyal governments in Southern Confederate states. He drew up his plans without calling Congress into a special session to help with the policy. First, Johnson appointed temporary governors in the states that had seceded. The governors would vote to deny any U.S. help in repaying their Confederate debts and would ratify the Thirteenth Amendment, which outlawed slavery. Second, he granted amnesty, or pardons, to all former Confederates, except top-ranking military leaders. Anyone who was not automatically given amnesty could apply directly to Johnson for an individual pardon.

Only people with amnesty or who had been pardoned could participate in the reconstruction of their state.

When members of Congress heard of Johnson's plans, they were outraged. Johnson's disregard for Congress's input insulted some members, who felt that Congress should plan the Reconstruction of the South. Under Johnson's plan, Southern representatives would be invited back into the House. Union members felt that the Confederate states should be treated like newly conquered territories and certainly should have no vote on new policies for the South. Even when House members confronted Johnson with their complaints, he refused to back down. Members immediately called a meeting to discuss how to stop the president from making any further decisions without the consent of Congress.

To these House members, known as the Radical Republicans, simple emancipation of the slaves was not enough to reconstruct the South. Furthermore, they thought, these traitors to the Union should not be allowed back in Congress so soon. The members knew, however, that the Southerners would reappear to claim their House seats at the Thirty-Ninth Congress in December 1865. House members scrambled to find a loophole so they could legally exclude the Southerners. They found one just in time. By law, the clerk of the House must take roll call before the session begins. Only names that are called can take part in business. The clerk could conveniently leave the names of Southern representatives off the list. In addition, in 1862, every member was required to take

Initially, many members of Congress were relieved that Andrew Johnson was the person who would succeed Abraham Lincoln as president. Johnson quickly issued two proclamations regarding the Reconstruction of the South without input from Congress. Johnson's action was the first of many that would place him at odds with Congress.

an oath stating, "I do solemnly swear that I have never voluntarily borne arms against the United States." Surely, no Southerner from a seceded state could take that oath.

The sun beamed brightly in the sky on December 4 as House members made their way to convene the Thirty-Ninth Congress. No doubt, the cheery weather pumped up the Radicals. Crowds of people flooded the Capitol, eager to watch the historic proceedings. As the session got going, the clerk started roll call. When he skipped over Horace Maynard, a representative from Tennessee, the puzzled member tried to question the clerk. The clerk shot back, telling the representative not to interrupt roll call. The representative piped down for the moment and patiently waited for the clerk to finish.

After roll call, one Radical quickly moved to elect the House Speaker. Business was starting without the Southerners. At this point, Maynard demanded that his name be added to the roll. Immediately, the House burst into an uproar. Radical Thaddeus Stevens jumped up and called for order, while the clerk shouted that he would not recognize any member not on his list. Boos echoed throughout the chamber. When the Radicals refused to add the members to the roll call, the Southerners had no choice than to get up and leave.

Over the next several days, the House heard speeches from those who condemned Johnson's plan to pardon Confederates and allow them back into office. If the representatives of the South were readmitted, they argued, freed slaves would be treated no better than captive slaves. Four million slaves were about to be set free, but without a cent or even a place to live. The laws of slavery had kept African Americans from getting an education, learning how to support themselves, or understanding laws of business. The House felt it was the responsibility of Congress to help these people start their new lives.

In dealing with the South, Congress stared at a devastated area of the country. Plantations were destroyed, transportation was wrecked, and once-great cities, like Atlanta, lay in ruins. Confederate soldiers returned from the war to find their homes burned to the ground, their farms leveled, and their families living in squalor. To fix these problems, Radicals wanted to redistribute the land among all Southerners. This solution would break up the power of large plantations and provide land for the freed slaves. The proposal, though, was too extreme for most of Congress, which swiftly defeated the bill.

Instead, Congress passed a bill that gave more powers to the Freedmen's Bureau, an agency formed in March 1865 to help distressed refugees of the Civil War. The bill allowed the Bureau to protect former slaves against discrimination. The legislation also would keep the Freedmen's Bureau working as long as it was needed and would help freed slaves in all parts of the country, not just the South. The bill was supported by moderates who felt they could work with the president to bring down "black codes" in the South. These laws discriminated against freed slaves and kept them from basic freedoms like

REVOLT IN THE HOUSE

★ ★ ★ ★ ★

Contention and conflict have been a part of the House of Representatives throughout its history. Another time trouble began to brew in the House of Representatives was when Republican Joseph G. Cannon was elected Speaker in 1903. At this time, the Speaker had almost complete control of the floor agenda. The Speaker chaired the Rules Committee, which held the power to allow or not allow bills onto the floor for debate and a vote. Therefore, Cannon was able to stop legislation he opposed. He also could attach amendments, or riders, to bills that on their own probably would not have passed a floor vote. Moreover, once a bill was on the floor, the Speaker could limit the time of debate. Cannon had a way of recognizing those representatives he wanted to and ignoring the ones he did not. Members quickly realized he had too much freedom to pursue his personal agenda.

Cannon was ruling the House with an iron fist. He used his array of powers for his own personal plans. Time and time again, he used control

owning property, living in town, public speaking, and other liberties promised in the Bill of Rights.

Much to the surprise of Congress, Johnson vetoed the bill. He reasoned that Congress had no right to pass such a bill with 11 states unrepresented. Moderates were stunned that the president would shoot down such a conservative piece of legislation. They offered another bill that granted civil rights to all people born in the United States, except Native Americans. It guaranteed rights to everyone, regardless of race. Those who violated the law would be put

to obstruct legislation, quash opposition, or favor certain bills. Instead of supporting the issues of his majority party, he herded a new majority, made up of members from both parties. The tension and frustration finally sparked a revolt in the House.

In 1910, during the Sixty-First Congress, House members struck back at Cannon's tyrant-like rule and came up with a resolution that slashed the powers of the Speaker. Cannon tried to fight back, calling the proposal "out of order." Nevertheless, representatives passed the Norris Resolution, a list of rules that limited the Speaker's control over the House. Under the resolution, the Speaker could no longer appoint committee chairmen and committee members. The resolution removed the Speaker from the Rules Committee and increased the number of seats on that committee from five to ten—six majority-party seats and four minority-party seats.

on trial and punished with fines or imprisonment. The bill easily passed in both houses.

Johnson vetoed this bill, too. His response was openly racist, doubting that blacks could qualify for citizenship and arguing that states had every right to discriminate on the basis of race. Both houses of Congress were enraged. All moderates who wanted to cooperate with Johnson felt insulted. The veto was seen as a declaration of war. It ignited a battle of butting heads between Congress and the president. The House passed the bill again and so did the

Senate, overturning Johnson's veto and making the bill a law. The Civil Rights Act was the first major law in American history to be enacted without the president's approval. For the next several months, Congress and the president sparred in showdown after showdown. Congress would pass legislation. Johnson would veto it. Congress would override the veto. As weeks ticked on, the fuse became shorter. Sooner or later, someone was bound to explode.

On January 3, 1867, the Military Reconstruction Act was introduced in Congress. It divided the South into five

OUTSIDE OF THE GALLERIES OF THE HOUSE OF REPRESENTATIVES DURING THE PASSAGE OF THE CIVIL RIGHTS BILL.

In this engraving published in *Harper's Weekly*, crowds celebrated outside the House of Representatives after the Civil Rights Bill of 1866 passed. President Johnson vetoed the legislation, and both houses of Congress overrode his veto. The bill was the first major law to be passed in U.S. history without the president's approval.

military districts. Commanders of these districts would have the power to maintain order, protect freed slaves, and assist in Reconstruction. The bill was passed in response to riots and violence taking place daily in the South. Hundreds of African Americans were being ruthlessly murdered by whites. Johnson vetoed the bill, but again Congress overrode it.

The following summer, Johnson decided to take action to interfere with military Reconstruction in the South. He began to remove officers from the military districts and to replace them with his own. When Congress found out about Johnson's actions, members started to reinstate the original commanders. Tired of Johnson's lack of cooperation, one House representative took the matter a step further. He motioned that Andrew Johnson, president of the United States, be impeached for high crimes and misdemeanors in office.

JOHNSON IMPEACHED

A heated debate ensued between Republicans and Democrats. Radicals went on a rampage, rattling off Johnson's past misdeeds, but they failed to point out any charges that would be "high crimes and misdemeanors." Democrats accused Republicans of stirring up a political coup. Nevertheless, on the afternoon of February 24, 1868, the House approved impeachment by a vote of 126 to 47. House members presented the Senate with a list of charges. These included violations of several acts that Congress had passed, the use of intimidation and threats to remove military commanders from their posts, and certain violent comments the president had made. The case went to the Senate for trial.

On March 30, the day the trial began, crowds packed the galleries of the Senate. The prosecuting lawyers, who were House members, rambled on about the president's offensive behavior. They declared that the country was in danger because of Johnson's king-like actions. They argued that Johnson was twisting the Constitution to serve his own agenda. At times, he acted as if some of its laws were no longer important. In other words, prosecutors accused Johnson of violating the Constitution and showing no respect to the supreme law of the land. Yet they offered no sound proof to support their charges.

When the prosecutors finished presenting their case, spectators jumped to their feet, shouting out cheers of approval. The chief justice pounded his gavel and demanded order. The crowd answered him with boos, hisses, and laughter. Immediately, the judge ordered that the galleries be cleared.

Next, the defense argued against the accusations and stressed that Johnson had not committed a crime that called for impeachment. Johnson's lawyers reminded the court that impeachment was a trial of law, not politics. Johnson may have been an unpopular president, but that did not mean he should be tossed out of office. They pleaded with the court to base its decision on the Constitution.

On May 16, the Senate voted 35 in favor of impeachment and 19 against it. Johnson was just one vote shy of the

Representative Thaddeus Stevens, one of the Radical Republicans, is shown closing the debate on the impeachment of President Andrew Johnson in the House. After the Senate voted to acquit Johnson, Stevens said, "The country is going to the devil."

two-thirds needed for conviction. House members were stunned. Some representatives hurled nasty objections. Radical Thaddeus Stevens threw his arms into the air and shouted, "The country is going to the devil." Enough members in the Senate had agreed with the defense that prosecutors were asking the court to make a decision based on politics. The court did not want to destroy the Constitution just to get rid of an undesirable president. Apparently shaken by the whole ordeal, Johnson served out the rest of his term without any more controversy.

6

HERE, THE
PEOPLE GOVERN

The work of Congress has been dramatic at times—
enacting the Bill of Rights or impeaching a president.
For the most part, though, House members simply attend
to daily business as usual. On a typical day, House members arrive at the U.S. Capitol in Washington, D.C., ready
for work. As they pass into the chamber of the House,
they see the words of Alexander Hamilton painted above
the doors: "Here, sir, the people govern." This phrase reminds members who the real rulers of the country are—
the American citizens. Once inside, each member takes a
seat either on the right side of the chamber or the left. At
one end of the chamber is a two-tiered rostrum, or a plat-
form used for public speaking. The Speaker presides from
the top tier. Clerks and other officers use the lower tier.

The oath of office is administered to members of the 109th Congress on January 4, 2005. As seen from the Speaker's chair, the Democrats sit on the right of the center aisle, the Republicans on the left.

The seats of the representatives are arranged in a semi-circle pattern in front of the rostrum. A wide central aisle divides the semicircle into two sections. By tradition, as viewed from the Speaker's chair, the Democrats sit on the right side of the center aisle and the Republicans sit on the left side. Otherwise, unlike U.S. senators, members of the House have no assigned seats.

As soon as the members are called to order, the chaplain delivers an opening prayer. After the opening, the Speaker of the House approves the Journal, a record of the previous day's proceedings. A representative may demand a roll-call vote to approve the Journal. Roll-call votes are cast using an electronic machine that holds the votes on record. Representatives scan their ID cards into one of numerous voting stations on the House floor. A screen then pops up that asks them to vote "yea," "nay," or "present." (A "present" vote is like a vote to abstain.) After approval of the Journal, a House member leads the chamber in reciting the Pledge of Allegiance, the same way many students start the school day.

The House then listens to messages from the Senate and news from the president, and grants committees the permission to file reports. Afterward, members can give one-minute speeches on any topic. Finally, the House turns to legislative business, breaking into its separate committees. Most committee work is performed by 20 standing, or permanent, committees. Each committee has jurisdiction over a specific field, like agriculture, health, education, or foreign affairs.

Standing committees consider, amend, and report bills that fall within their field. When it comes to bills, committees have tremendous powers. They may block legislation before it even reaches the House floor. Standing committees also oversee the departments and agencies of the executive branch. These committees have the power to hold hearings and to subpoena witnesses and evidence. Each committee may also have several subcommittees. With some exceptions, members of the House may serve on only two committees and four subcommittees. Members usually seek election to a committee that covers a field in which they are most qualified and interested. Each committee has a professional staff to assist in its work. For standing committees, the staff is limited to 30 people.

Besides the standing committees, the House also has a Committee of the Whole, which, as its name suggests, consists of all members of the House. The committee was created to move legislation quickly to the House floor for debate, by eliminating some transitional steps. The Committee of the Whole meets in the House chamber, where it considers and amends bill but it may not pass them. Once the process of discussing and amending a bill is complete, the Committee of the Whole dissolves. The House can then vote on the amendments recommended by the committee and on the final bill.

After committee work or other legislative business is done for the day, members may speak for up to 60 minutes on any topic. Because the House is formally adjourned, other members are not required to stay and listen. Often, speakers talk to a nearly deserted chamber.

Typically, the House meets for business on weekdays. Sessions on Saturdays or Sundays are rare. Most sittings of the House are open to the public and are shown live on television by C-SPAN. Although a typical day in the House may appear a bit humdrum, plenty of excitement and prestige can be involved in making laws for the country.

BECOMING A MEMBER

Every summer, Americans celebrate the Fourth of July, or Independence Day. Most people associate the

BEHAVIOR ON THE HOUSE FLOOR

The Pocket Guide of Floor Procedure in the House of Representatives, prepared by the Rules Committee in 2001, offers "Rules of Decorum and Debate." According to some of the rules, members of the House shall:

- Address their remarks solely and directly to the chair. They may not address other members, individuals in the gallery, or persons who might be observing through the media.

- Refer to other members by state, not by name.

- Avoid characterizing another member's intent or motives and discussing personalities.

- Refrain from using profane or vulgar language.

- Refrain from speaking disrespectfully of the Speaker, other members, the president, or the vice president.

- Refrain from eating, smoking, or using electronic equipment, including cellular phones or laptop computers, on the floor.

- Wear appropriate business attire. Hats and overcoats are not permitted on the floor.

Fourth of July with backyard barbecues and fireworks. Some people might even recall the courage of American colonists, who declared their independence from Great Britain and fought a war to guarantee it. Independence Day, however, is more than just a celebration of winning the Revolutionary War. It is a time to celebrate the revolutionary idea of a government ruled by the people. The American Revolution was led by the belief that in a legitimate government, the people are sovereign, or the ultimate rulers. Under this concept, neither Congress nor the president has the power. The power belongs to the people.

The House of Representatives is working proof of this idea. When the founders wrote the Constitution, they wanted House members to come from among the people. Therefore, qualifications to serve in the House were kept simple. Candidates must be residents of the states they plan to represent, at least 25 years old, and U.S. citizens for at least seven years. Also, House members only serve two-year terms. If a representative is not doing what the constituents want, the people can elect someone else. In this way, Americans are guaranteed a fair voice in government.

On the other hand, the Senate was designed to serve a different purpose. Originally, the Senate consisted of a group of wise politicians and businessmen who were not directly bound to the people. Instead, each state legislature chose its senators. Also, senators serve longer, six-year terms. In 1913, the Seventeenth Amendment changed the way senators were elected. Today, senators are elected directly by the voters in each state. Therefore, both the House and the Senate work for the American people. The Senate serves as a system of checks and balances for the House. Hot legislation—coming directly from the passions of the people—has a chance to "cool down" with the Senate. The Senate can review bills and help decide whether they would be good laws.

How exactly does the House represent the people? As stated earlier, House representation is based on population. The original Constitution stated that each member of the House must represent at least 30,000 people, and each state must have at least one representative. As the nation's population rises and shifts, states gain and lose congressional representation. Every 10 years, a census is taken, and the count helps decide the number of representatives. In the first Congress, the House seated 65 representatives from the 13 states. As time passed, new states joined the Union, and the country's population increased. As a result, the House added seats. By 1913, its membership had grown to 435. No doubt, the population would keep growing, and the House would keep adding members. Congress saw trouble ahead. If the House got too large, the members would not be able to do their jobs efficiently. So Congress passed a law that limited the number of House members to 435. If Congress had never passed this law, the House would now have more than 1,000 members. Today, there is one representative for about every 630,000 people in the United States.

The last census was taken in 2000. After this census, some states gained representatives; other states lost a representative or two. The following list shows the changes:

Arizona	+2
California	+1
Colorado	+1
Connecticut	-1
Florida	+2
Georgia	+2
Illinois	-1
Indiana	-1
Michigan	-1
Mississippi	-1
Nevada	+1
New York	-2
North Carolina	+1
Ohio	-1
Oklahoma	-1
Pennsylvania	-2
Texas	+2
Wisconsin	-1

These changes went into effect the following election year, which was 2002, and stay in effect until after the 2010 census. The population of the United States continues to grow steadily, and most of that growth is in the South and West. Four states in the Sunbelt gained two seats apiece, while two states in the Northeast lost two seats and several others there and in the Midwest lost one seat.

Interestingly, a dispute arose between the states of Utah and North Carolina about which state would gain a seat. Utah claimed that out-of-state Mormon missionaries should have been counted as Utah residents in the census.

State representatives also argued that the use of "imputa-tion" was unconstitutional. This practice occurs when a census taker cannot reach anyone at home. In these cases, the census taker estimates the number of people living at a residence. Imputation increased North Carolina's popula-tion more than it did Utah's; if imputation had not been used, Utah would have gotten the extra seat. The case went to the Supreme Court in March 2002 as *Utah v. Evans*. (Donald Evans was the secretary of commerce at the time, and the 2000 census was conducted by the Department of Commerce.) On June 20, 2002, the Supreme Court ruled against Utah. Until the next census, North Carolina has 13 representatives, and Utah has three. If Utah had won its claim, it would have had four representatives, while North Carolina would have had 12.

In addition to the 435 representatives from the states, the House has four nonvoting delegates. One delegate comes from each of the following: the District of Colum-bia, Guam, American Samoa, and the U.S. Virgin Islands. Puerto Rico also sends a resident commissioner. The del-egates and resident commissioner have the right to vote in committees on which they serve, but they cannot vote on matters before the entire House. Some proposals have been put forth in recent years to allow the delegate from the District of Columbia to be a full voting member.

BREAKING DOWN THE HOUSE

For the most part, the 435 members of the House, the four delegates, and Puerto Rico's resident commissioner come

Eleanor Holmes Norton *(left)*, the nonvoting delegate from the District of Columbia, met in 2001 with Condoleezza Rice, who was then the national security advisor. Many residents of Washington, D.C., would like to see the delegate become a member of the House with full voting privileges.

from the two major political parties—the Democratic Party and the Republican Party. Republicans favor themselves as traditional conservatives—they support lower taxes, a limited government role in economic issues, and government intervention in some social issues. Democrats are generally considered more liberal—they back social freedoms and an economy tempered by government intervention and believe that government should play a role in alleviating social injustice. Besides these two main parties, numerous smaller parties participate in the political process, like the American Independent Party, the Reform Party, the Green Party, and even the Socialist Party. The party that has the most seats in the House is considered the majority party. The other party becomes the minority.

The Speaker, or the highest-ranking and presiding officer, is elected by the House of Representatives, and since the majority party has more members, the Speaker is typically a member of that party. In the 110th Congress, Democrats hold the majority in the House, so the Speaker is Democrat Nancy Pelosi of California. Pelosi is the first woman to be Speaker. Generally, no other member of Congress gets as much recognition and authority as the Speaker. The Speaker is next in line behind the vice president to succeed to the presidency. In other words, if both the president and the vice president died or were impeached while in office, the Speaker of the House would become president.

The Speaker's most important deputy is the majority leader, the majority party's floor leader. House representatives elect their leaders—including the majority leader—by secret ballot in their party caucuses, or conferences, before the beginning of each new Congress (every two years). Cooperating with the Speaker, the majority leader works to achieve the party's legislative goals. The majority leader also holds a top seat on the Budget Committee.

Minority parties also have a leader—the minority leader. These members promote unity within the party. They also

When Representative Nancy Pelosi was elected the minority whip by Democrats in 2001, she received a ceremonial whip from David Bonior, who previously held the office. The whip for each political party works to encourage party discipline within the ranks. Pelosi became Speaker of the House in the 110th Congress.

form alliances with members of the majority party who share their views about certain issues. It has been said that the minority leader has two main jobs—to keep the party together and to look for votes on the other side.

An assistant to the majority or minority leader is called a whip. Whips encourage party discipline, or "whip members into line." They persuade party members to vote for legislation, encourage attendance, gather information about how members are planning to vote, and use this information to persuade people to vote a certain way. The whips also have several deputy whips, assistant whips, or regional whips to help them in their duties.

With so many members in the House of Representatives, sometimes leaders like the whips are needed to keep order. More than 400 minds don't always think alike. Yet, cooperation is often seen in the House, especially when it comes to the process of turning a proposal into law.

7

From Bill to Law

Proposed legislation may come from a variety of sources—a representative from the House, a member of the president's Cabinet, the president. Businesses, public interest groups, or trade associations may help draft bills. Constituents may request a bill, too. Sometimes, a House member will introduce a bill "by request," even if he or she does not personally support the proposal. Yet it's not necessarily easy to turn an idea into a law. During each two-year term of Congress, about 15,000 bills and resolutions are introduced in the House and Senate. Of those, only about 600 become public laws.

In the House, representatives introduce a bill by dropping it in the "hopper," a box on the clerk's desk. The member who introduces the bill is known as its primary sponsor, and an unlimited number of representatives may be cosponsors. The clerk assigns the bill a number.

A bill originating in the House is designated by the letters "H.R." followed by a number. There are two types of bills—public and private. A public bill generally affects the population at large. A bill that affects an individual or private entity instead of the general public is a private bill. A typical private bill is used in matters like naturalization and immigration. The bill is then forwarded to the appropriate committee or subcommittee. For important bills, committees and subcommittees set a date for a public hearing. The date, place, and issue to be discussed are published as a public announcement in the *Congressional*

Attending a House Homeland Security Committee meeting in June 2006 were *(from left)* Mayor Anthony Williams of Washington, D.C., Mayor Michael Bloomberg of New York City, and Police Commissioner Raymond Kelly of New York City. The hearing was held to discuss homeland security funding cuts for Washington and New York.

Record. After a hearing in a subcommittee, the panel usually considers the bill in a mark-up session. During the mark-up session, the bill is discussed and analyzed. At the end of the debate, members take a vote. If the majority votes in favor of the bill, the legislation is referred to the full committee.

When the full committee sees the bill, it may vote to release the bill to the House with a recommendation to pass it. Releasing the bill is called reporting it out. In reporting a bill, the committee staff writes a report explaining the bill and its purpose. The committee may report the bill without amendments, or it may make changes to the legislation and present it as a "clean bill," with amendments. A committee may also table a bill or not take any action on it. If a bill is not reported by the end of a Congress, it dies.

If a bill is reported, it goes to one of five House calendars. The Union Calendar takes all bills that have anything to do with the Treasury—bills that raise money or request money. Bills on the House Calendar are usually administrative and procedural issues and do not address money. The Corrections Calendar is for bills that focus on changing laws, rules, and regulations that are judged to be outdated or unnecessary. A bill on the Corrections Calendar needs a three-fifths majority to pass. The Private Calendar holds bills that deal with individual matters, like claims against the government or special requests from immigrants. Finally, the Discharge Calendar is not a list of bills, but rather of petitions or motions to release a

A BILL BEGINS ITS PATH

Thousands of bills are introduced during each term of Congress. One such bill in 2006 was H.R. 5145, introduced on April 6 by Representative Walter B. Jones, Jr., a Republican from North Carolina. According to a summary of the bill, it would authorize "the National War Dogs Monument, Inc. to establish in the District of Columbia a monument to honor the sacrifice and service of United States Armed Forces working dog teams."

In a press release, Jones said, "Over the course of our nation's military history, those who have bravely served our country in battle have been recognized and remembered for their loyalty and sacrifice. In that tradition, one breed of hero has been too often overlooked. Tens of thousands of war dogs served our nation during World War I and World War II, and in Korea, Vietnam, the Persian Gulf, Bosnia, Kosovo, Afghanistan and Iraq."

The bill, which had four cosponsors, was referred to the House Committee on Resources. Comment was requested from the U.S. Department of the Interior. On April 18, the bill was referred to the Resources Committee's Subcommittee on National Parks. The subcommittee held hearings on June 22. No further action has been recorded.

legislative committee from considering a bill any further. Usually, a majority of House members must sign the petition before it will be placed on the Discharge Calendar. Some bills on the House and Union calendars are more important than others. The Rules Committee decides which bills should be considered first.

Often, before bills are considered by the entire House chamber, they come before the Committee of the Whole. All measures on the Union Calendar must first come before the Committee of the Whole. The committee debates and amends the bill. To help move the process along, the Committee of the Whole requires only 100 members for a quorum instead of the normal House quorum of 218 members. After the Committee of the Whole finishes its debates, the bill is presented to the full House.

Most of the time, votes are decided by a simple majority, except in special cases. Some bills need a two-thirds majority vote. These bills include constitutional amendments, those to override a veto from the president, and those to expel members. There are four ways to vote in the House: a voice vote, in which the chair asks for "ayes" and "nays" and decides the winner by volume; a division vote, in which the chair asks the "ayes" and "nays" to rise separately, then counts them; a teller vote, in which members pass between designated "tellers" who count them and announce the results to the chair; and a recorded vote, in which members use an electronic voting machine. A recorded vote must be requested by a member and have the approval of one-fifth of the quorum or 25 members of the Committee of the Whole. If a recorded vote is approved, it has priority over the first three procedures.

If a bill is passed by the House, the legislation moves to the Senate. The Senate can either pass it or kill it. When passing legislation, however, the Senate often adds its own amendments. In that case, a joint House-Senate conference committee must meet to reconcile the differences between the bill passed in the House and the one passed in the Senate. If there is no consensus, the bill dies. If consensus is reached, the bill goes back to both chambers for approval.

Once the House and Senate approve the bill as presented by the conference committee, the legislation goes to the president to sign. The president can approve and sign the bill, making it law; veto (or reject) the bill and return it to the Senate or the House, whichever originated the legislation; or do nothing. If the president does nothing, the bill becomes law after 10 days. If Congress adjourns during the 10-day time frame, preventing the president from returning the bill with his objections, the bill does not become law. This situation is called a "pocket veto."

If the president vetoes a bill, the actions taken by Congress determine what happens next. If two-thirds of the members present in both the House and the Senate pass the vetoed bill, it becomes law, even though the president has vetoed it. If the House and the Senate do not respond, or if not enough members vote to pass the bill, it dies. Congress can then try to rewrite the bill to make it more acceptable to the president or give up on the legislation.

The House also passes resolutions, which are motions that cannot be voted into actual law. For example, the House may vote on support for U.S. troops in Iraq. The vote carries no legal weight. Instead, the resolution is more for moral support than a motion to take legal action.

SERVICE TO THE PEOPLE

The creation of our nation's laws is perhaps the most important way that a member of the House of Representatives serves the people. A representative, though, and the staff in his office also provide an array of other services to those who live in their districts.

Residents can contact their representative's office if they have questions or are having problems in dealing with a federal agency. Although representatives and their staff members cannot overrule decisions made by a federal agency, they may be able to intervene on a person's behalf to get questions answered, resolve problems, or cut through the red tape. Caseworkers in a U.S. representative's office are regularly in contact with federal agencies, including the Social Security Administration, the Internal Revenue Service, U.S. Citizenship and Immigration Services, the Department of Veterans Affairs, and Medicare and health-care agencies.

The federal government offers thousands of grants that an organization, like a school group or a nonprofit agency, may be eligible to receive. A representative's office may be able to help such groups find grants they could qualify to receive. Sometimes, too, a representative will write letters of support to go along with the grant applications. Information on federal grants and loan programs for businesses is also available through a representative's office. And a

House member's Web site may offer further information on topics like how to start your own business.

Assistance is also available for constituents who may not even be old enough to vote. High school students may be interested in attending one of the nation's service academies. These are the Air Force Academy, the Naval Academy, the Military Academy (West Point), the Merchant Marine Academy, and the Coast Guard Academy. For the first four academies, students who wish to be considered for an appointment must meet eligibility requirements and

During induction day at the U.S. Naval Academy, a group of plebes, or freshmen, read *Reef Points*, a book that covers midshipman slang, the academy's mission, and its history. To be admitted to one of the country's service academies, a student must be nominated by a U.S. representative or a U.S. senator.

be nominated by an authorized person—usually a U.S. representative or a U.S. senator. Members of Congress take their responsibilities in nominating students to the various academies seriously. Appointments to the Coast Guard Academy are made based on a nationwide competition. Many representatives also offer internships to high school and college students in their Washington offices as well as at their offices back in their districts.

Through their representative's office, people can purchase a flag that has flown over the U.S. Capitol in Washington. Arrangements can be made for the flag to be flown on a specific date. That way the flag could be given as a way to honor someone on a special day. Certificates come with each flag to indicate for whom it was flown and for what occasion.

People who are planning to visit Washington, D.C., on vacation may contact their representative's office to arrange for tours of the White House and the U.S. Capitol, as well as other government offices and sites like the U.S. Supreme Court, the Bureau of Engraving and Printing, the Library of Congress, the National Cathedral, and the National Archives.

8

COMMITTEES

Committees are the backbone of the U.S. House of Representatives. A bill will probably receive the most attention when it is in committee, and committees are where the public gets a chance to be heard. In most cases, in order for a bill to have any chance of passage, it must be reported favorably out of the committee to which it was assigned. So, committee work is an important part of the legislative process. Not all committees are created equal, though. Among the most powerful and prestigious committees in the House are the Rules Committee and two committees that have to do with money: the Appropriations Committee and the Ways and Means Committee.

Unlike most other committees, the Rules Committee is not responsible for a specific area of policy. Still, it is one of the most important committees because it is responsible for determining the rules under which other bills will come to the House floor for consideration. The committee is sometimes referred to as "the traffic cop" for the House. The Rules Committee has 13 members, with nine from the majority party and four from the minority party. This ratio reflects the committee's role as an arm of the leadership that controls the House.

When a bill is reported out of another committee, it goes to the Rules Committee. The committee decides what will be allowed during the debate of the bill on the House floor. For example, if the leadership wants to attract attention for a piece of legislation, the committee may allow time for long speeches in support. On the other hand, if the leadership wants a bill to receive little notice, the committee may schedule no debate time.

Rules of another sort fall under the jurisdiction of the Committee on Standards of Official Conduct, which is often called the Ethics Committee. The panel has many functions, but all of them concern rules that cover the ethical conduct of members of the House. These rules govern areas like gifts, travel, treatment of staff, and conflicts of interest. The committee investigates possible violations and recommends whether action should be taken against a representative. Such punishments could include censure (an official expression of disapproval) or expulsion from the House.

MONEY MATTERS

The Appropriations Committee is in charge of setting the federal government's expenditures. The basis of the committee's power is in its ability to spend funds, and as the federal budget has grown, so has the committee's clout. Openings on the committee are in demand, and appointments are often used as rewards. Appropriations tends to be a less partisan committee than other panels, since members of both parties have an interest in ensuring that legislation contains spending for their own districts. The committee is one of the largest in the House.

The House Budget Committee oversees the federal budget process and reviews all bills and resolutions on the budget. It also oversees the Congressional Budget Office, a nonpartisan agency that provides economic and budgetary analysis to Congress.

If the Appropriations Committee oversees the spending of federal money, the Ways and Means Committee is the panel that handles the raising of money. The Constitution says that all bills regarding taxation must originate in the House of Representatives. All taxation bills go through the Ways and Means Committee, and for this reason, the panel is particularly powerful. The Ways and Means Committee also has jurisdiction over a number of entitlement programs, including the Social Security program, which provides retirement and disability benefits, and the Medicare health insurance program.

A position on the Ways and Means Committee is a coveted one, especially because it has jurisdiction over a wide range of policy issues. Members of the House want to be on the committee just so they may have some influence over policy decisions. Among the issues that have gone through the committee in recent years are the tax cuts put forth by President George W. Bush; a prescription drug benefit for Medicare recipients; and welfare reform. The Ways and Means Committee was established in the first Congress in 1789, though it existed for only eight weeks. After that, taxation bills were

U.S. Defense Secretary Donald Rumsfeld *(right)* spoke with U.S. Representative Jerry Lewis *(center)* of the House Appropriations Committee in February 2004 before the committee's meeting on the Department of Defense budget. In 2005 and 2006, Lewis was chairman of the Appropriations Committee, one of the more powerful panels in the House.

COMMITTEES WITH THE SENATE

In addition to the standing committees in the House and the Senate, Congress has four joint committees that include members from both bodies. Bills are not referred to the joint committees; therefore, their power is considerably less than that of the standing committees.

The Joint Committee on Taxation has 10 members: five from the House Ways and Means Committee and five from the Senate Finance Committee. This joint committee investigates the administration of the tax system and studies measures and methods for the simplification of taxes. It reports on its investigations. The Joint Economic Committee also issues advisory reports. The main task of this committee is to review economic conditions and recommend improvements in economic policy.

The Joint Committee on the Library oversees the Library of Congress, as well as the U.S. Botanic Garden and the congressional art collection. The fourth panel, the Joint Committee on Printing, oversees the Government Printing Office, which prints and provides access to documents produced by and for the three branches of the federal government.

taken up by temporary committees until a permanent Ways and Means Committee was created in 1802.

Ways and Means may have had its roots in the first Congress, but the oldest continuous committee is the Energy and Commerce Committee, which was originally formed as the Committee on Commerce and Manufactures in 1795. Similar to Ways and Means, the Energy and Commerce Committee has a broad sphere of influence. The committee oversees legislation relating to telecommunications, consumer protection, food and drug safety, public health, air quality and environmental health, the supply and delivery of energy, and interstate and foreign commerce in general. This jurisdiction extends over five Cabinet-level departments and seven independent agencies.

Dyan French, a New Orleans community leader, testified in December 2005 before the Select Bipartisan Committee to Investigate the Preparation for and Response to Hurricane Katrina. The panel was a special committee set up for a limited time by the House of Representatives. The House also has 20 standing, or permanent, committees.

The House has one permanent committee that is not considered a standing committee—the Permanent Select Committee on Intelligence. This committee oversees the intelligence community in the United States, including the Central Intelligence Agency (CIA), the Federal Bureau of Investigation (FBI), the Department of Defense, and the Department of Homeland Security. This committee, however, does share some jurisdiction with other committees in the House when dealing with matters of the Department of Defense and the various branches of the U.S. military.

The remaining standing committees in the House are Agriculture, Armed Services, Education and the Workforce, Financial Services, Government Reform, Homeland Security, House Administration, International Relations, Judiciary, Resources, Science, Small Business, Transportation and Infrastructure, and Veterans' Affairs.

The House also can create select committees to serve for a limited time or purpose. After completing its assigned task, such as investigating a government activity and writing a report, the committee often dissolves. The House, however, can extend the existence and authority of the committee. An example of such a panel was the Select Bipartisan Committee to Investigate the Preparation for and Response to Hurricane Katrina. The committee was established in September 2005 to investigate and study the responses to Hurricane Katrina and report its findings to the House by February 15, 2006.

9

On the House Floor

Each two-year term of the U.S. Congress is called a "Congress." Over the years, Congresses have been numbered, beginning with the first Congress in 1789–1790. A Congress begins on January 3 of odd-numbered years and has two regular sessions—one each year. Thousands of bills are discussed each session. Bills have a wide range of topics. In the 110th Congress (2007–2008), bills in the House ranged from ending the war in Iraq to detaining possible terrorists living in the United States to honoring war veterans to building a national war dogs monument. The Constitution requires Congress to publish its proceedings. The House publishes a Journal, which lists the simple, basic reports of chamber proceedings. The

Congressional Record publishes every word that is spoken on the floors of the House and Senate and includes all roll-call votes on all questions.

Throughout U.S. history, the appearance of the House has dramatically changed. In the beginning, House members were mainly white men. Since then, more minorities and women have become representatives. In 1967, only five African Americans held House seats. By 1993, there were 38 African-American members, 16 of them from Southern states. By 2007, that number had risen to 42. In 1995, just 19 Hispanics held seats in the House, but in 2007, there were 27 Hispanic members. The same is true for women in Congress. The number of women in the House went from 11 in 1965 to 48 in 1993 to 71 in 2007.

By percentage, however, the 435 representatives today do not match the percentage of women, African Americans, Hispanics, and Asian Americans in the U.S. population. The 2000 census found that women made up 50.9 percent of the population, but in the House, they hold only 16.3 percent of the seats. In other democracies around the world, women are represented in much larger numbers. The same problem exists for minorities. African Americans make up 12.3 percent of the population but only 9.66 percent of the House. Likewise, Hispanics make up 12.5 percent of the population but hold just 6.2 percent of House seats.

On the brighter side, House proceedings are much more open today than they were years ago. The public is

Members of the Congressional Black Caucus of the 109th Congress held a swearing-in ceremony on January 4, 2005, at the Library of Congress. Back in 1967, the House of Representatives only had five African-American members.

encouraged to visit the House and learn what is happening on the House floor. Spectators often fill the galleries and listen to the debates.

DO-NOTHING CONGRESS

People often like to make jokes about a "do-nothing" Congress. Sometimes it seems as if congressional representatives just twiddle their thumbs, bicker, and never get any work done. Many people think legislators are just a bunch of crooks who spend too much money and lie to the public.

Over the years, Congress has enacted an array of legislative gems that have made the United States a safer country and a better place to live. It all started in the First

GET INVOLVED

★ ★ ★ ★ ★

Think you are too young to be a part of your government? Think again. Start being active right now, and you will grow up to be a valuable citizen of this country. Here are some ways to get involved with Congress.

Learn more about Congress. You have taken the first step just by reading this book. There are many more ways to bolster your knowledge of the government. Read newspapers, watch the news, or pick up a few current-events magazines, like *Time*, *Newsweek*, or *U.S. News and World Report*. Use them to learn all about what is happening in Congress today. Visit a few of the Web sites listed at the end of this book. Becoming politically smart will help you make informed decisions about the people you will support and vote for someday.

Voting is the most important way to get involved. It is your right, and many people worked hard to earn that right for you. To vote in state and national elections, you must be 18 years old and a U.S. citizen. For now, you can find other ways to help "rock the vote." Encourage your family and friends to exercise their right to vote. If you hear someone say, "My vote doesn't matter," remind them that the Constitution says

Congress with the Bill of Rights. Thanks to this piece of legislation, every American enjoys basic civil rights. People can voice their opinions without being thrown into jail or beaten. All Americans have the right to practice whatever religion they choose without being arrested or persecuted. Basically, you can make your own decisions about how to live your life, thanks to a law created by the House.

otherwise. In fact, many elections have been very close races, right to the finish.

Meet your member of Congress. When your representative is in town, show up and try to shake his or her hand. Maybe you can think of a good question to ask. Remember, your representative cares about what you think. If you cannot meet your representative in person, write him or her a letter, a postcard, or an e-mail. You can find addresses on the United States House of Representatives Web site at www.house.gov.

Don't want to be the only one taking action? Talk to your friends and get them involved, too. It is more fun to work together as a group. Maybe your school or community is having a problem your representative should know about. You and your classmates could write a letter together asking for help and sign your names to the petition. Representatives count on their constituents to keep them up to date on important needs or local priorities. The Constitution guarantees your voice in Congress. Take advantage of it.

From time to time, some major event takes place that reminds people just how much they depend on the U.S. government. For example, after the Oklahoma City bombing in 1995 and again after the September 11 terrorist attacks in 2001, public support for Congress and the federal government rose to all-time highs. On days like these, the role of Congress becomes engraved in people's minds.

Congress, though, has a much greater impact on everyday life that often goes unnoticed.

For starters, did you wake up to an alarm clock this morning? If you live in a rural area, you can thank the 1936 Rural Electrification Act, which brought electricity to farm homes. Likewise if you live in the city, congressional regulations keep electricity flowing to your house or apartment at a price you can afford. Once you are out of bed and brushing your teeth, recall the 1974 Safe Drinking Water Act, which set standards for drinking water—free of deadly chemicals and bacteria. Also, makeup, vitamins, and prescription drugs are all regulated by Congress to make sure they are safe for you to use. When you sit down at the breakfast table to eat your bacon and eggs, remember that the Department of Agriculture—working with policies set by Congress—makes sure that those products stand up to tough inspections so that you don't get sick from eating them.

The House of Representatives has had a hand in many other great laws. In 1843, Congress helped provide funds to Samuel Morse (inventor of the Morse code) to develop a telegraph between Washington, D.C., and Baltimore, Maryland. This system laid the groundwork for modern telecommunications networks. In 1916, Representative Edward Keating and Senator Robert L. Owen became appalled at the widespread use of children as workers in factories. The Keating-Owen Act was the first federal effort to end child labor. As chair of the House Committee on Labor, Representative Mary Norton of New

Traffic moves through the Interstate 85-Interstate 285 interchange in Atlanta, Georgia. The Federal Interstate Highway Act marked its fiftieth anniversary in 2006. The law, passed in 1956, set aside $25 billion for the construction of 40,000 miles of interstate highways.

Jersey pushed to pass the 1938 Fair Labor Standards Act, setting the first national minimum wage. In 1956, Hale Boggs of Louisiana and George Fallon of Maryland presented the Federal Interstate Highway Act. This legislation set aside $25 billion for the construction of more than 40,000 miles (64,375 kilometers) of interstate highways. Representative Edith Green of Oregon is often called the "mother of higher education." She helped pass the Higher Education Act of 1965, which created the federal student aid program. This law has given millions of students the chance to attend college.

Sometimes, the "dark side" of government may get more attention. From its very beginning, however, the goal of Congress has always been to employ honest representatives. Back in 1787 and 1788, James Madison (who would later become the fourth president of the United States), Alexander Hamilton, and John Jay wrote the *Federalist Papers*, a series of 85 articles that persuaded states to ratify the U.S. Constitution. In number 57, Madison wrote that the goal of every political constitution should be to first find legislators who possess wisdom to make good decisions and virtue to pursue the common good of the society. Next, he said, they should do all they can to stay trustworthy. Today, most House members try to live by this job description. Almost all members understand that it is a great honor to represent the American people in government and strive to continue a more than 200-year-old tradition of upholding the Constitution.

GLOSSARY

abolish To do away with completely.

abstain To refrain, as from a vote.

amnesty The act of a government by which pardon is granted to a large group of people.

caucus A closed meeting of a group of people belonging to the same political party or faction, usually to select candidates or decide on policy.

census An official, usually periodic, count of the population and recording of such data as economic status, age, sex, and more.

coup The sudden, forcible overthrow of a ruler or a government by a small group of people already having some political or military authority.

emancipation The freedom of people from bondage, servitude, or serfdom.

inauguration The formal induction of an official into office.

incumbent The person who holds a political office.

legislation A draft of a law proposed to a lawmaking body.

nationalist An advocate of national independence or a strong national government.

quorum   The minimum number of members required to be present at an assembly or meeting before it can proceed to conduct business.

ratify   To approve or sanction formally.

Reconstruction   The process after the Civil War of reorganizing the Southern states that had seceded and re-establishing them in the Union.

resolution   A formal expression of opinion, will, or intent voted by an official body or an assembled group.

secession   The act of withdrawing or separating; in U.S. history, the withdrawal of the Southern states from the federal Union at the start of the Civil War.

sovereign   Of or holding the position of ruler.

Speaker of the House   The presiding officer of the House of Representatives.

subpoena   A written legal order directing a person to appear in court, or also to appear at a U.S. House committee hearing to testify or supply specified documents or records.

treaty   A formal agreement between two or more countries, relating to peace, alliances, trade, or other issues.

unconstitutional   Not in accordance with or permitted by a constitution, specifically the U.S. Constitution.

veto   The power of the president to refuse to sign a bill passed by Congress; the bill is prevented from becoming law unless it is passed again with a two-thirds majority by both houses of Congress.

whip   A member of a legislative body appointed by a political party to enforce party discipline and to secure the attendance of party members at important sessions.

BIBLIOGRAPHY

Cohn, Mary W., Ed. *How Congress Works*. Washington, D.C.: Congressional Quarterly Inc., 1991.

Davidson, Roger H. and Walter J. Oleszek. *Congress and Its Members*. Washington, D.C.: Congressional Quarterly Inc., 1990.

Galloway, George B. *History of the House of Representatives*. New York: Thomas Y. Crowell Company, 1961.

Goehlert, Robert U. and Fenton S. Martin. *Congress and Lawmaking: Researching the Legislative Process*. Santa Barbara, Calif.: ABC-Clio Inc., 1989.

Hamilton, Lee H. *How Congress Works and Why You Should Care*. Bloomington, Ind.: Indiana University Press, 2004.

Kessler, Ronald. *Inside Congress: The Shocking Scandals, Corruption, and Abuse of Power Behind the Scenes on Capitol Hill*. New York: Pocket Books, 1997.

Remini, Robert V. *The House: The History of the House of Representatives*. New York: HarperCollins Publishers/Smithsonian Books, 2006.

Web Sites

United States House of Representatives
www.house.gov

FURTHER READING

Dewhirst, Robert. *Encyclopedia of the United States Congress*. New York: Facts on File, 2006

Hamilton, Lee H. *How Congress Works and Why You Should Care*. Bloomington, Ind.: Indiana University Press, 2004.

Ritchie, Donald A. *The Congress of the United States: A Student Companion*. New York: Oxford University Press USA, 2001.

Web Sites

Ben's Guide to U.S. Government for Kids
bensguide.gpo.gov

FirstGov for Kids
www.kids.gov

Kids in the House
http://clerkkids.house.gov

The National Archives Experience: The Constitution of the United States
www.archives.gov/national-archives-experience/charters/constitution.html

Thomas: The Library of Congress (Legislative information from the Library of Congress)
http://thomas.loc.gov

The United States House of Representatives
www.house.gov

PICTURE CREDITS

INDEX

ABOUT THE AUTHOR

RACHEL A. KOESTLER-GRACK has worked with non-fiction books as an editor and a writer since 1999. During her career, she has worked extensively with historical topics, ranging from the Middle Ages to the Colonial era to the civil rights movement. In addition, she has written numerous biographies on a variety of historical and contemporary figures. Rachel lives with her husband and daughter on a hobby farm near Glencoe, Minnesota.